A QUIET UNFOLDING

DAWN LANUZA   LAYLA S. TANJUTCO
KB MENIADO   ALLONAH GACUTAN
DOMINIQUE GONZAGA- SULATRA
KRING TALLADEN   LAKAN TULA
ROMY PEÑA CRUZ

A SOFT LANDING.

CONTENT WARNING

This book explores the themes of death, grief, coping with loss, abuse in the family, and talk of body image and appearance.

If you feel the need to take a break in between these pages, please do.

We support caring for yourself during this reading experience.

INTRODUCTION

In December 2022, I flirted with the idea of building a community of Filipino poetry enthusiasts. This idea was from my desire to find kindred: people who share the same interest and love in reading, writing, and creating poetry books.

I started *a soft landing.* because I genuinely believe that more poets in the Philippines are not being read, are still budding in the craft, or are in need of a bigger platform or means to produce their work yet.

I was once them. I started out my writing career not knowing that I would be in this space. For me, poetry has always been intimidating, but falling in love with it as a reader first, and an attempted poet next, has done wonders for my mental and emotional health. It has bettered my craft and has widened my audience of readers through the years.

Of course, I didn't do all of it alone.

My success after releasing my very first poetry book in 2016 was met with love and support by my existing readers and community. But it grew so much more than I've ever anticipated or expected, reaching readers from countries I've never been to.

I will always attribute this success to four things: readers, editors, community, and intuition.

As a member of a writing community (#romanceclass), I learned that while writing can be a solitary endeavor, it is so much better to do it with a group of like-minded folks with similar goals and aspirations to lift you as you go through your phases as a writer.

I started *a soft landing.* with what I believe every writer needs, no matter where they are in their careers: editors and readers. I've tapped my editor and beta reader, Layla and KB, in this journey, confident that whatever I build will be in good hands with their knowledge, skill, experience, and empathy.

In my nine (going on ten!) years of being a published author, I have learned the importance of having a team, and I would like to replicate that experience for *a soft landing.* to make sure that the people we find feel supported and empowered as they launch themselves further into their writing careers.

If you liked any of the authors featured in this collection, I hope that you support them in their next endeavor.

May you find inspiration in this collection, recognize the talent in each of these writers, and continue to support Filipino poets and authors.

Happy reading!
Dawn

All these stories we've been writing together
i sure hope u don't become a stranger

—LAKAN

KISHŌTENKETSU

If my life had structure
I want it to be like
kishōtenketsu.
Not everything has to be about
battles and victories
for beautiful things
still come out of
quiet unfolding.

HUDBAS

i'm bad with names but it's different with you
hella heart eyes coz u seem good at what you do
mixture of bad and good, boy, you don't take cues
you know how to treat me better, more when it's just us two

i know i wouldn't find a better lover
wouldn't fall in love another summer
all these stories we've been writing together
i sure **hope u** don't become **a stranger**

MY FAVORITE PLACE

My favorite place
can be anywhere

Sure, maybe somewhere with clear skies,
blue waters, strong trees, flowers in bloom

Or, maybe somewhere with lots of laughter,
unabashed hand holding, tight hugs, loud love

But really, my favorite place
can be anywhere

Just somewhere happiness thrives
Somewhere dreams come true

FREE TO BE

a tiny house
on a farm
of my own
would be neat

a space
to grow
to think
and to sit

with people
i call mine
or by myself
would be fine

as long as it's a place
where tiny means free—
free to live large or wild
or even just to be.

A NEW HOME

When you found me, I had been lost for ages I'd forgotten what it was like to be found, to have a home. But you took my hand and sat me down. Laid flowers at my feet. Showered me with kisses and so much love I didn't know what to do with it at first. I had to relearn a language I once knew but had no one to speak with and so the words faded until you taught them to me one by one. Until I began to speak in a tongue only you and I could understand. You brought me into this strange new world I did not know existed. I did not think it was possible but you woke me up from a nightmare when I did not even know I was asleep. And for that, I would be forever thankful, forever yours.

You took my hand
and sat me down.
Laid flowers
at my feet.
Showered me
with kisses
and so much love
I didn't know
what to do with it.

—Layla S. Tanjutco

IF MY COUNTRY WAS A PERSON

Here we have:
Those who remember,
Those who chose to forget.

If my country was a person,
I would tell her: go to therapy.
Talk about the things that hurt.
Don't bury them because
you are too ashamed of the crimes
you yourself caused.

The bodies you witnessed:
Missing, then found dead.
Floating in a river,
wrapped up in tape.

The sins that you failed to identify:
The people who convinced you
it was justified.

The occurrence that made you think
it was all right.
The silence that you chose:
The fear they instilled in you.

The sharp breath you took
watching other people,
convinced that it could never be you.

But it is.

You are a moving target.
Dead man walking.
The sound of the clock
ticking *you, you, you.*

If my country was a person,
I would tell her,
a fucked up thing would keep happening until you say,
enough.

Look at you, pretending that your resilience is not just abuse
in a mask.

BEFORE FLYING

There is no waking up
from a night of no sleep,
with excitement seeping in
from somewhere so deep

Checking and rechecking,
afraid of forgetting something
The pain of needing to return
too many times learned

There is no backing out
from a seat sealed for months,
prepared for queues and scans
where it can take forever to stand

Cold floors, makeshift mats
Every minute important to catch
Impromptu snacking, rushing feet
Always waiting to pass through the gates

There is no getting away
from wanting to get away
There is no judgment
for those wanting to stay

Waiting, adjusting
Changing, replacing—
Impossible becomes possible
Here, where coming and going is okay.

FAT

Experts say I need
To lose half my weight
To reach the ideal size
Why do I need to be
Less of me
To be considered
Acceptable
Enough and
Deserving of
Love?

TENTH OF MAY

I don't know how to hold you through this pain
My arms feel weak and I am also afraid
Let me be the quiet,
the stillness,
the space you can be in
at this moment.

TIME TO COME

Even misery eats the strongest
Yet faith will never fail
Might one falls a thousand times more
Shall it make them any less?
Overpowering doubt may prevail
Still light can shine through
Hollowness and heaviness fade
Comfort welcomes with embrace

THE ANTIDOTE

I've been trying to make you
love me again
for half our lives,
it's the poison I needed to cure.

That whole time,
I had the antidote in my hands.
I could have just dosed love on myself
enough to understand,

Your love does not weigh more than mine.

There
is
no
judgment
for
those
wanting
to
stay.

— KB Meniado

WHY I STARTED WRITING
AFTER NAOMI SHIHAB NYE

I began writing because I was wearing too thick of a sleeve
for my skin and I couldn't bear the stiffness of not scratching
the itch a minute more. I wanted to peel off the shame and
sink my teeth underneath the sins of my fingernails. I
wanted a taste of this raw bleeding thing. I wanted to wipe
the crevices of my eyes and deep dive into the acidic chyme
of my stomach, to grab the shovel and find the hatchets I
promised to bury but swallowed whole instead. I wanted to
see if the lesions were still breathing, if the views over my
shoulder were still worth the visit, or if the back of my
tongue was still sticky with being 12-and-wishful, or 17-and-
stupid, or 23-and-sad. I began writing because breakfasts
were boring and I'd rather chew my own cheeks grimy with
cheap talk and knockoff psyche. I began writing because I
wanted to walk around the maze made of my shivering
bones and give handshakes to my long-lost frequencies I
failed to call in return.

WEEDS: A CAUTIONARY TALE

as with any plant
the weed starts as a seed
dropped by a bird on a field
or cast by a worm
burrowing deep into the earth
where the seed
upon finding itself
in the dark warm depths
awakens and

s t r e t c h e s

its limbs toward open air
it will find itself
in the company of others
who, though may mirror its image,
were deliberately planted where they grew

the weed will see its neighbors
billow gently in the summer breeze
as they grow golden in the sun

when the hands that planted the weed's neighbors
fail to uproot the growing scourge,
the weed will grow bolder

the weed,
alone and lonely,
will shake itself once, twice
scattering seeds all around
so that it may soon shimmy with other weeds
for they grow fast and are hardier
and stronger than their neighbors

when the storm comes
the weeds will stand tall,
their roots deep into the ground
while their neighbors, bowed by the wind,
and the heaviness of their grains,
bury their golden tips in the black mud
unable to rise again

the weed, from but a tiny seed
that found itself in a large rice field unseen and unchecked,
can multiply so that one day
all its neighbors will have vanished
and only the weeds will remain

MY CHILD

my hurt little child, that time will be the last
i apologize for letting your voice get lost in the crowd
forever shall i pay for neglecting you in the past
i vow to strive for the best and make you proud

THE LAST PETAL

Pink was the color of her cheeks when she told them she was leaving; the color of the late afternoon sky when she ran home crying; the color of her father's shirt when he opened the door, eyes searching; the color of the decade-old kitchen mantel she stared at, recalling everything.

Pink was meant to be the color of her dreams fulfilled; of when she would finally feel enough; of no more fighting. But it was that same pink that tainted her—*"one mistake too many"*—fingers and pens pointing, scribbling, blaming.

Pink was the color of the bougainvillea in the garden staring back; the color of the shame in her heart, screaming; the color of solace as her father's hand reached for hers, holding her as if she were the last petal about to fall.

LIFE ON HAND*

light hits
hands clench
some warmth
palms stretch

first touch
arm flex
firm grip
wrist checks

hard times
good times
fingers tap
veins pop

knuckles fail
bones frail
last hold
stay bold

THE BEACH

Remind me how it feels
to have the sand beneath my
feet be dragged by the
ebbs of the sea.
To breathe in the salt
and breathe out my worries
Feel the gentle wind against my face
Make me believe
I could fly far from here.

Remind me how it feels
to not have every piece
of me tremble every time I breathe.
I've been bracing to grow out
of this frayed and ragged skin,
It's been way too long,
I need to be brand new.
I'm here to pick up my ruins
and make a castle out of me.

WALK WILD

we all have our time;
we peak at our perfect timing,
when we do, we're freed from
what held us back.

they may have barred the windows,
and locked the doors,
but it doesn't stop:
flowers from blooming,
flamingos from soaring.

if we want to feel love,
we must get out of the house.
explore the wonders of the wilderness.
and heal our inner child.
grow up,
stand up.
walk wild.

this is the end of the poem.
But not the end of me.

— Kring Talladen

PAUSE. PRAY. WRITE.

When will *these* end?

Daily chores like waterfalls,
Taxing tasks like flash floods
Backaches like tidal waves
My heart's longings like a surge

I pause,
so I can breathe
and not drown.

I pray,
so I can surrender
to the Flow.

I write,
so I can float
as me, for me.

Whenever the cycle turns,
I fetch these three steps in a bucket

until the water does not hurt anymore.

This is the end of the poem.
But not the end of me.

BETTER DAYS*

With hopes of battling fear
In old memories
We float
All the whys and the what-ifs
"When is this all going to end?"
Dreams, they spill over
As waves rush to shore
We sink in the sand
The horizon casts
"If better days are coming, then
what's taking them so long?"

~

"If better days are coming, then
what's taking them so long?"
The horizon casts
We sink in the sand
As waves rush to shore
Dreams, they spill over

"When is this all going to end?"
All the whys and the what-ifs
We float
In old memories
With hopes of battling fear

I'm still trying
to be okay
at the thought
of you
never arriving
at my front door
no matter
how green I light
my porch.

—Allonah Gacutan

NEW ADDRESS
AFTER CLEMENTINE VON RADICS

I'm here on a bench in
the middle of a new city.
I find comfort at the thought that
these pavements have
never seen your footprints.
Here, you're not real,
just a thought that floats,
a cloud that dissipates
once the wind whips me back
to this city's artificial meadows.

Here, I'm just trying to be a girl
who can drink milkless coffee,
wash the day-old greasy dishes,
parallel park my '03 Camry,
do a cat eye with one stroke,
and doesn't cry at words like
"I don't see myself with you".

Here, I buried our possibility
beneath my apartment floor
where I pace barefoot 'til I'm breathless;
legs weak, ears pinned to the ground
to hear the muffled creaking of
our could-have-beens pounding for oxygen.
Here, I'm still trying to be okay at
the thought of you never arriving
at my front door no matter
how green I light my porch.

IYAKIN

Did we all grow up thinking that crying was a sign of weakness? We used to tease each other in school when someone started to tear up, even when we could see they were in pain.

As an adult, I had to relearn crying: it is not a weakness; it is release.
And what a relief it is!
To allow my body to breathe or to let go of what it's been holding back or holding on to.

Some days we're due for a good cry.

Think: *how freeing it is to empty myself so I can fill up with good again.*

THERE WAS NO JOY TO BE FOUND IN THE SHADOWS

a wounded animal,
hurt but alive,
will find the deepest,
darkest cave.
there it will stay
to nurse its wounds
and keep itself safe:
a fearful prey.
time heals all wounds,
that's what they always say
and in due course, the animal
will seek the light of day.
so there is no reason
not to take the leap
it's time to leave
the shadows
and come out
of the deep and dark cave

the wounds have healed
scars are all that remain
out there is sunlight
it's a brand new day

I have found
the hands
that know
how to hold me.

—Dominique Gonzaga-Sulatra

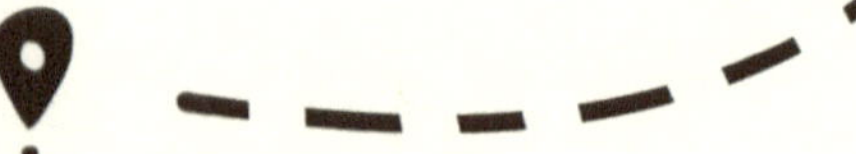

NOT BLINDLY AND NEVER FORGETTING

My father's hands were huge.

Enough to cover my entire cheek. Strong enough to protect.

But also big and hefty enough to bring damage and chaos around me.

Growing up, I did not understand how the same hands I've seen do a multitude of good things were the same hands that caused my mother to lose her smile.

How the same hands that carefully carried me as a child were the same hands that had inflicted bruises and scars in my life.

Make the good things matter, he would always remind me.

But what does one do when the person who says good things is the same one who causes the bad?

They say the same hands that hurt can never be the same hands that heal.

I choose to forgive him anyway.

Not blindly. Forgive but never forget.

With the passing of time, moving forward is possible. A different kind of strength arose when I learned to accept that the ones we love can hurt us and leave us. Piece by piece, I put myself back together. And from grace to grace, healing began.

I have found the hands that know how to hold me gently, the shoulders that I can lean on anytime, and the heart that loves and knows me unconditionally.

The memories are still there, vivid as day. But they no longer sting. They have no more power over me. He has no power over me. And every time I see my father, I put my hands together in prayer.

May he learn to forgive himself too.

GRACE

Unforgivable, they said—
the pain he caused from my childhood.
To be abandoned at a time of great need
was the most hurtful of all.

But I rushed to him years later,
when I was told he was sick.
It took days for me to arrive north,
long enough for him to fetch me
at the blue and white bus station.

The day was ending and the first stop
was a supper for two, then a trike ride
to the seashore near his house.
The orange sunset welcomed us
as our feet made prints on the sand.
The coconut trees danced with the wind
and said hello to our shadows
that suffered from distance and disdain.

The gap has closed since then,
not much with words but with actions:
lunch dates that fill both the soul and stomach,
corny jokes that turn the frown into a smile,
catch-ups and stories that calm the mind.

What led to forgiveness, I'm not sure.
I guess it's true that "time heals all wounds."

But I believe more in grace—
Grace that can only come from the Divine,
Grace that overflowed from what I first received.
Grace that only the undeserved deserve.

A HOPEFUL AFTER

Life has been thrice divided
into befores and afters

The first was when I saw him last
as his body was placed into the ground
Head shaking, heart shattering
Oblivious of what was to unfold

The second was when I got lost in the forest
driving until I could not see the road
Mind racing, heart pounding
thoughts scattered like stars in the dark sky

The third was when a tiny hand
wrapped around my finger
Eyes tearing, heart swelling
grateful for that December in the South

That was when all the grief
started to melt away
and the anger I used as a shield
cracked and fell to the ground

I hold on to the hope
that in trying to raise her well
it will stop the maddening cycle

And from here on out
bury the sorrow
and let only love foster

I hold on to the hope
that in trying to raive her well
it will stop the maddening cycle.

— Romy Peña Cruz

SELAH

dust settling
hope fading

days dragging
hearts drowning

in tears, in fears
in doubts so big

they towered over us,
over everything

curtains not shut
but light still out of reach

and then

twin maroon lines on a stick
a sweet, rhythmic soundwave

a black-and-white thermal piece of paper
a blinking dot on a screen

like a ray of light
seeping through a dark room
there you were

you came along,

bringing hope
carrying light

illuminating, radiating
giving us life through yours

GROWTH

when you want something to grow
you have to plant the seed
and wait
let some rain fall
allow it to see the rays
of the sun
time will take care
of the rest

i heard it works
for plants too

A LETTER WHISPERED TO THE WIND

One day I whispered a letter to the wind.
Stamped it with a prayer for a life well-lived,
hoping the birds carry my message to you
for whatever the future holds

I recalled the night I cried
for my words and actions
said and done out of spite
That is why I wished to do what was right

As I stared at my toddler picking olives
from the pizza about to go stale,
I thought,
Wasn't that what happened to us?
Should I have sent my letter in the mail?

The sun continued to rise
The world went on to turn
And now I am starting to find peace
should our paths never cross again

So when you happen to be
on my mind once more
I will be sure to remember
my letter whispered to the wind

ALL GOOD THINGS COME WITH EXPIRATION DATES

The thing about rust is that it spreads over time
it runs through the walls until things start to fall apart.
We couldn't tell where it started, or where the root of the
problem was.
We had to go around and inspect.

When we talk about the things we never said,
did they still pierce you?
I've carried it around so much that it almost felt like
poking a fresh wound.

Talking about it is a time machine.

I learned that feelings could be like
preserved fruit.
We store it in jars, keep it at the back
hoping that by the time we remember,
it would still taste good.

But all good things come with expiration dates,

and that includes me and you.
Here I am, looking at you,
knowing that this love is past due.

This love lived with me
but never met you.

WORTHY

Someday, well into the future, I hope you will look back to this time in your life and remember I was a small part of it, even for a little while. That I was there when you needed me, that I did my best, and gave you my all, because it was no less than what you deserved. I hope someday when you've finally done what you've set out to do, you will think back fondly at us and what we were able to do. How I was to you. What I had been. And what I had not. What you had been to me and what you had not. We could have tried harder, could have made it work better, could have done things differently. You could have chosen us. I could have fought to beat all the odds to have things our way. But. I hope for no more regrets because life is too short and people really do come and go. And though I had wanted to stay, and you did not want me to go, we have come to accept that our chapter together must come to a close, eventually.

When we become the strangers we once were to each other, I hope we will both remember to simply be grateful for being able to be what the other needed and wanted at that particular time in our lives. I know I am thankful for everything you taught me about truly loving someone, of having fear clutch one's heart and going in just the same because in the end, it was all worth it. You were all worth it. I know I was.

SOLO

I sit in a diner at a table good for four, and you look at me and the L-O-N-E-L-Y tangled in my hair like it's being too loud. You don't notice how the loneliness sits primly with its shoulders back now. Loneliness looks different now: it could drag my pale untrained limbs to the other part of this city; five-kilometer-walk for a cup of iced specialty coffee. It unpacks and organizes the moving boxes left unopened from three breakdowns back. It washes the well-kept dusty porcelain sets for casual taco-and-wine Wednesdays. It waits quietly for sunrise and sits bravely in a park at night.

Loneliness - I can now hold its face with both of my shaky hands without my body decomposing at its touch.

SELF-APPOINTED

I don't think of it as a flaw anymore.
I just come out right at the cage and say,
"These are my scars,
and I'm trying not to pick on them."
I'm trying to heal
and sometimes it's not perfect.
I used to be afraid of being picked
apart but that was before
I gathered all of my pieces.
I am mine to reassemble,
to complete as a whole.
I am no one's project but my own.

EDITORS' NOTES

It started with a concept and a love for poetry. When Dawn told me her idea of publishing a collection of poetry featuring new (or newish) poets at the start of 2023, I was immediately on board and excited. Dawn then asked KB, who also said yes. The three of us are based in different provinces across the country—Pangasinan, Quezon, and Davao—thought we had enough practice from the pandemic to take this little project from concept to execution without ever physically being together. Several Zoom calls, group chats, Google docs and worksheets, poetry prompts, close to a hundred emails, and a whole year later —here we are. And here it is, the maiden collection of *a soft landing.*

When we were talking about the concept of this collection, we tried to come up with a theme that we would focus on and landed~ on healing. Of all types and variations. After all, we are all still reeling from the pandemic and have lost so many—people, careers, things we hold dear. If we weren't already, the last three years had broken us in one way or another. We believed "healing" was an appropriate topic that would resonate with many people.

Luckily, when we put out the call for submissions, five other people agreed. We encouraged them to submit multiple works, and they did not disappoint. We were amazed not just at the obvious talent and skill, but at the diversity of the submissions. Each poet had their own style and distinct voice, which was amazing and brilliant. The poems we eventually selected showcased each poet's individuality while staying true to our theme. But. We were also putting together a collection that should make sense as a whole. It was also very challenging to determine the order in which the poems would appear to make a somewhat coherent story, and we got stuck here for weeks. As I was drafting this, we were still undecided about which of the two versions of the sequence we would use. (Also, work and personal health issues got in the way, as they do.) But you're reading this right now, so it would seem we finally figured it out.

Now on to the next collection. Where should we land next?

- Layla

Poetry can be intimidating, and writing and reading it are two different things. There's dealing with the economy of language, the cadence of the verses, and the sense of duty to follow and expect structures. There's also a myriad of interpretations, the weight of the messages, the translation of emotions and stories.

Then, there's editing poetry. When Dawn Lanuza asked me and Layla S. Tanjutco to join the *a soft landing.* team, one of the first things I did after saying yes was to bump up my to-be-read poetry pile. I wanted to study more about styles, trends, and forms, with the expectation of reviewing submissions by both fresh voices and those already well-versed with verse.

But the thing with poetry is, while indeed daunting, it can just be as simple as "what works" and "what feels." What works rhythmically? What feels straight-from/to-the-heart? What works effectively and what feels right? I'm grateful to be once again working with Dawn and Layla as we explore what makes up meaningful poetry and an equally meaningful collection, and honored to be learning from this first batch of wonderful poets—all through *a soft landing.*

And what a launch this is. In it, each piece is a representative of the theme of healing—from looking at one's self and own grief ("SOLO," "my child") and handling losses and acceptance ("A Hopeful After," "Pause. Pray. Write.") to mending hearts and ties ("Not blindly and never forgetting") and holding up and hoping ("If My Country Was A Person;" "there was no joy to be found in the shadows;" and "free to be"). Each piece is representative of its poet's story and voice, unique in its journey and yet familiar in its universality. Each piece works on its own and all together as one.

So, enjoy *A Quiet Unfolding*. Begin wherever you want. Pause and continue anytime you want. Find yourself in some of the lines. Let these poems land softly in your heart.

- KB

APPENDIX

POEMS BY DAWN LANUZA

- kishōtenketsu
- If My Country Was A Person
- Tenth of May
- Antidote
- iyakin
- all good things come with expiration dates
- self-appointed

POEMS BY LAYLA S. TANJUTCO

- A New Home
- Fat
- weeds: a cautionary tale
- there was no joy to be found in the shadows
- growth
- Worthy

POEMS BY KB MENIADO

- my favorite place
- free to be
- before flying
- time to come
- the last petal
- life on hand*
- better days*

** Two poems are a reverse poem. Reverse poetry can be read forward (top to bottom) or backward (bottom to top).*

POEMS BY ALLONAH GACUTAN

- Why I Started Writing
- The Beach
- New Address
- SOLO

POEMS BY DOMINIQUE GONZAGA-SULATRA

- Not blindly and never forgetting
- Selah

POEMS BY KRING TALLADEN

- Pause. Pray. Write.
- Grace

POEMS BY LAKAN TULA

- hudbas

- my child
- walk wild

POEMS BY ROMY PEÑA CRUZ

- A Hopeful After
- A Letter Whispered to the Wind

ACKNOWLEDGMENTS

From Dawn:

Big thanks to Layla and KB who said yes to this idea and for being the best partners for this project. Thanks for filling in the gaps and pushing on with me. :)
Grateful also for the authors who submitted during our Call for Submissions, the people who participated during our weekly prompts, and supported *a soft landing.*
To Alls, Nikka, Kring, Lakan, and Romy for sharing your voice to *a soft landing.*
To the revolution that is the Pink movement, for showing me what loving your country means.
To Shira, Shadow, Sage, and Pepper for all the pet cuddles.
To Hyunwoo, for saving 2023 by coming back.

From Layla:

My sincerest gratitude to Dawn, who plucked this project from her brain and trusted KB and I to help turn it into reality; to KB, I learned a lot from your insightful and helpful comments; to the authors—Allonah, Kring, Romy, Dominique, and LAKAN—whose brilliant talent shone through their submissions, thank you for trusting us and agreeing to join us in our little project; to Vy for the art inside, which are super awesome; to Carla, for our gorgeous cover, it's really the best; and to our friends at #romance-class, always grateful for your support and encouragement. Looking forward to the next collection.

From KB:

May my heartfelt gratitude soar high and land softly on: Dawn and Layla; Allonah, Dominique, Kring, LAKAN, Romy, and everyone who supports *a soft landing.*; my family; my all-time faves and inspirations; people who believe in what I can do; and, above all, God.

From Allonah:

I would like to thank the *a soft landing.* team for making this happen! The poetry writing community on Instagram, thank you so much for being the best source of so much inspiration and drive. My partner, Ike, who's usually the first person I read my poems to. My mama and papa, thank you so much for letting me be who I am. My friends, thank you for reading!

From Dominique:
Dawn, Layla, and KB, for holding space for my heart and poems
Harold, for always believing in me

Selah, for making me a mother
and God, for seeing me through it all

~

From Kring:
My overflowing gratitude to Dawn, Layla, and KB of *a soft landing.* for the help in improving my poems and for the opportunity to share new pieces to poetry enthusiasts. Thanks to my family and friends who believe in the poet in me. Above all, I'm grateful to God who gives me the grace I need to pursue this poetic path.

~

From LAKAN:
I would like to thank my chosen family; those who root for my happiness and those who stick with me in my unstable tendencies. The pen of LAKAN would not be continuously writing if you haven't pushed me to tell important stories—you all inspire me to keep going.
This is for Bim, my inner child who I once let down. From now on, you'll live loudly because no muting will happen with me by your side.

~

From Romy:
I would like to thank the team behind *a soft landing.* for making this book possible. To Dawn, Layla, and KB, you made a dream come true. KB, you've always been my cheer-leader and I am grateful we met in that EnviSci class. Love

Team forever! To Niña, for the messages and video calls that bridge the distance. To Jay and Arya, you are my whys. I love you. This bucket list item is also in honor of my late Dad, who had always believed in me.

ABOUT THE AUTHORS

Dawn Lanuza writes contemporary romance, young adult fiction, and poetry. She started to self-publish in 2014 with her debut romance novel, *The Boyfriend Backtrack*, which was eventually published by Anvil Publishing. In 2016, she also self-published her first poetry collection, *The Last Time I'll Write About You* which debuted at #1 on Amazon's Hot New Releases and stayed on its Bestsellers chart for over a year before it was re-released into an expanded and revised edition by Andrews McMeel Publishing. Two more poetry collections followed while she continued to write romance, choosing her favorite member in every boyband as a child raised by MTV. She loves music, pop stars, and creating imaginary scenarios with them.

Layla S. Tanjutco is a published author, and has edited over 30 works of fiction and poetry since 2014, many of which have been in local and international bestseller lists. She has written for TV, radio, corporate clients, and political campaigns during her career that spans over two decades and has a full-time career as writer and editor for two multilateral financial institutions.

KB Meniado is a reader, creator, and editor from the warm and beautiful Philippines. At age six, she fell in love with stories—finding them, creating them, sharing them—and hasn't looked back since. Her first published poem that appeared on the school paper was about smorgasbord, a word her seven-year-old self had just learned. Little did she know the piece would later lead her to a seemingly endless smorgasbord of creative projects...such as *a soft landing.*!

KB also runs Bookbed, a Filipino book community, and is a member of several reading and writing advocacy organizations. Find her at @heykebe online.

Allonah Gacutan is a 28-year-old human being who likes computers, coffee, long walks, Taylor Swift, and all things nice. She was born and raised in the beachside towns of La Union and spent some university years in the chilly city of Baguio. She's currently residing in Makati City, where she does remote work as a Business Intelligence Engineer. Allonah created an Instagram account (@allonah.g) last January 2020 to reconnect with her love for poetry and where she also posts some of her works. She started writing in high school, where she learned to love writing about young love and teenage heartbreaks. Today, she enjoys writing about life, self-discovery, nature, love, and heartbreak in all its different forms.

Dominique Gonzaga-Sulatra is a wife, mom, author, and editor based in Metro Manila, Philippines. Her life purpose is to be a good steward of her words and her growing family —two gifts she is most thankful to God for. In 2022, she released her first self-published book entitled *In the Breaking and the Becoming*. She is currently working on her second book and enjoying life changes with her husband and their firstborn, Selah.

Kring Talladen is a writer, editor, and poet. She serves full-time in the production department of a Catholic publishing company, while creating content for *Poetry Pauses* on Instagram (@poetrypauses) and Substack. She was a poetry fellow at the 2nd Amelia Lapeña-Bonifacio Writers Workshop in 2017 which focused on young adult literature. In December 2020, she self-published and launched her first poetry collection, *Parts and Personifications: 40 Poems of Letting Go*.

Based in Iloilo City, **LAKAN** is a self-confessed silent bragger that finds comfortability in writing poetry. Discovering at an early age his fondness of things that rhyme at the end, he aspired to become someone who writes such stuff confidently. May it be poetry or rap, he enjoys everything that rhymes and carries deep and important messages. Evolving from a phase of writing about naïve love poems, to now including social narratives in wording poems, it's safe to say that LAKAN's ideas in writing progresses as he ages. He has been published on *Novice Magazine x Creatives with Leni's* **Kulay Rosas ang Bukas Volume II: Panahon ng Paruparo** as a contributor, and is the author of the zine **Survival Sadness**, published in 2022. You may find him in these spaces:

Facebook: LAKAN TULA
Instagram: @lakan.tula
TikTok: @lakan.tula
Email: lakantula.ph@gmail.com
Website: lakantula.uwu.ai

Romy Peña Cruz is a freelance lifestyle and entertainment writer. She was a senior staff writer for YES! Magazine and a copyeditor for PEP.ph. A stay-at-home wife and mom currently based in Saudi Arabia, she is working on publishing her first romance novella. She started writing poems when she was 10 years old.

ABOUT THE ARTISTS

Vy Lin is a self-taught artist, a content creator, and an aspiring writer. Her full-time work revolves around website creation, design, and development but her passion for art remains. If not in front of a screen, she is creating in a cozy cafe. Her recent artworks explore modern calligraphy, vector, and outline art. Vy's goal has always been to visualize the words within and to share it with the world.

Carla de Guzman is bad at poetry, but loves a good journal session and a cup of coffee. Creating the cover for this collection was easy and familiar, and in a lot of ways, a nice place to be. You can find her making more art for Magdamag Market Cafe, or journaling and writing @carlakdeguzman.

www.ingramcontent.com/pod-product-compliance
Lightning Source LLC
Chambersburg PA
CBHW031327130726
47988CB00007B/3020